peaceful piano solos

a collection of 30 pieces

ISBN 978-1-5400-3963-7

Visit Hal Leonard Online at
www.halleonard.com

World headquarters, contact:
Hal Leonard
7777 West Bluemound Road
Milwaukee, WI 53213
Email: info@halleonard.com

In Europe, contact:
Hal Leonard Europe Limited
1 Red Place
London, W1K 6PL
Email: info@halleonardeurope.com

In Australia, contact:
Hal Leonard Australia Pty. Ltd.
4 Lentara Court
Cheltenham, Victoria, 3192 Australia
Email: info@halleonard.com.au

American Beauty

Theme from *American Beauty*

Words & Music by Thomas Newman

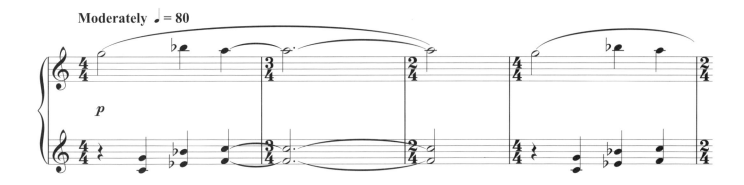

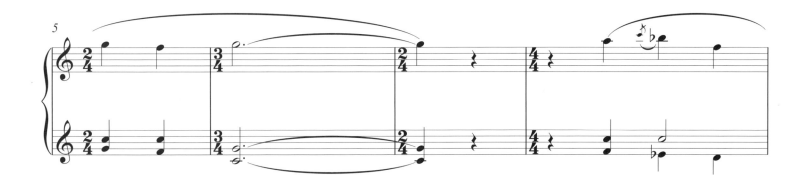

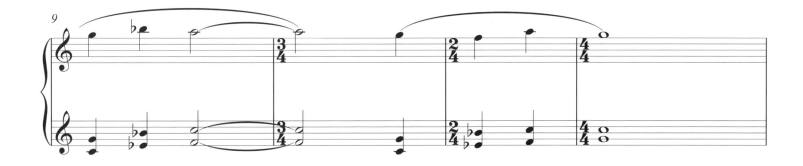

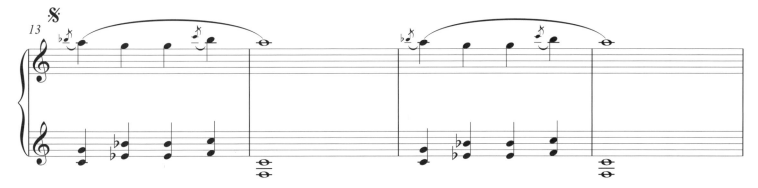

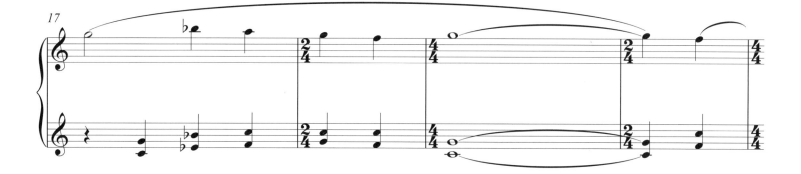

To Coda ⊕

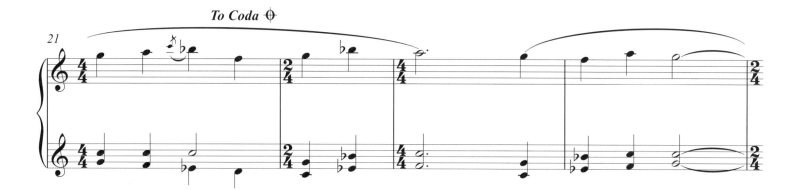

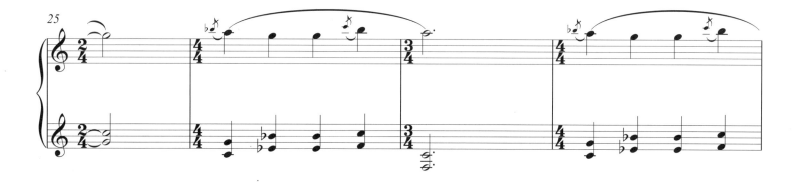

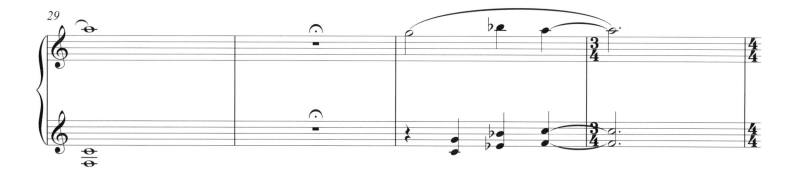

3

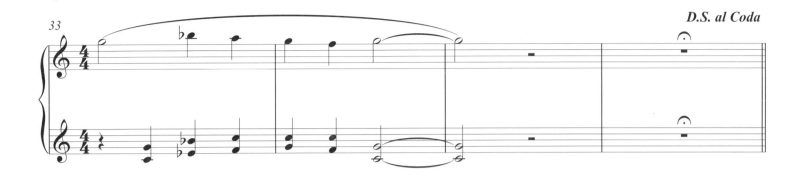

⊕ Coda

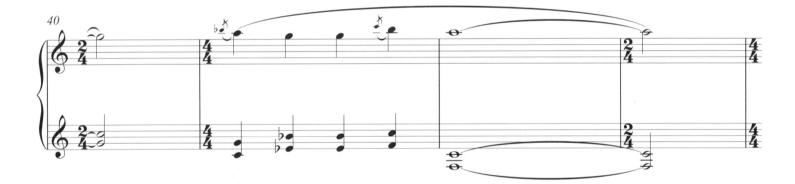

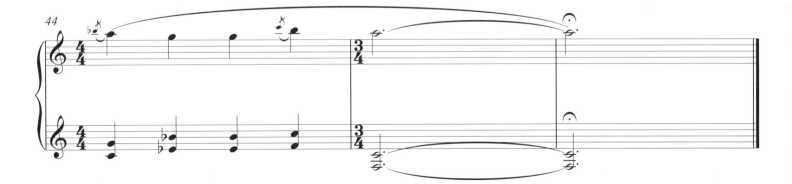

Big My Secret

from *The Piano*

Music by Michael Nyman

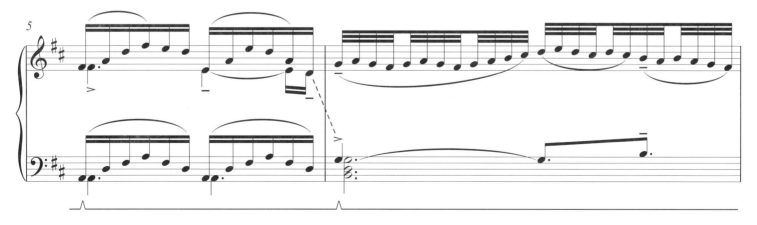

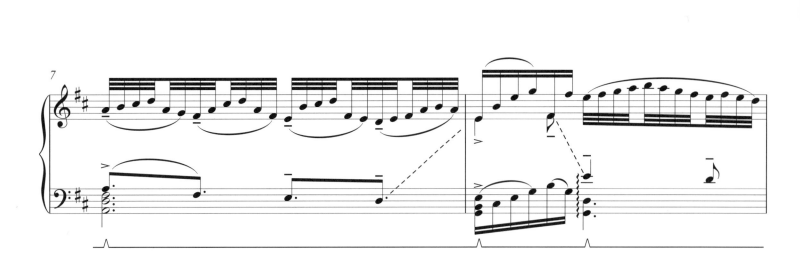

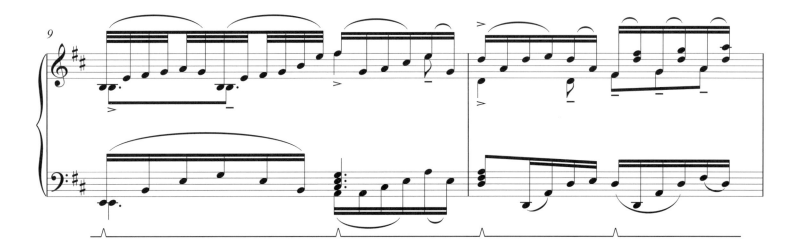

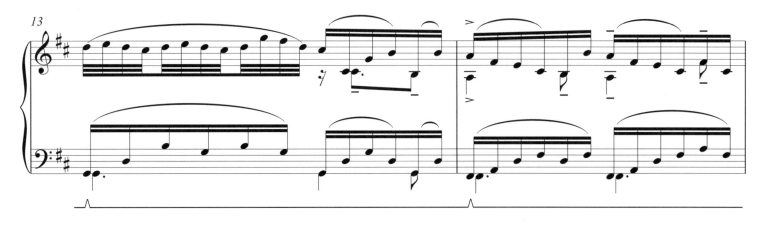

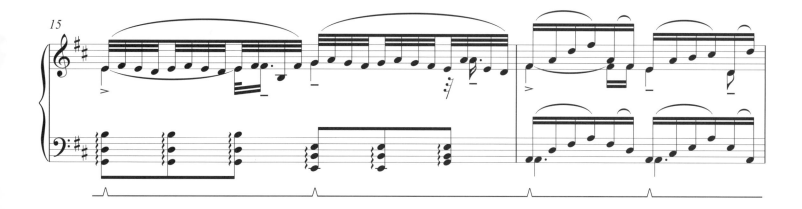

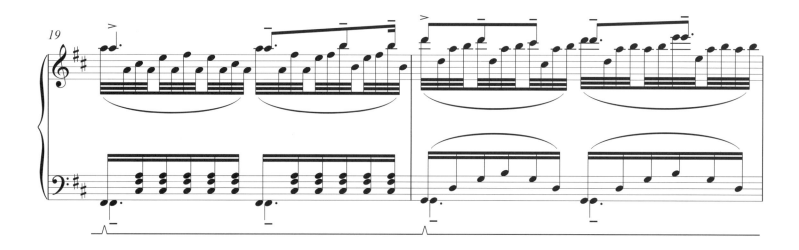

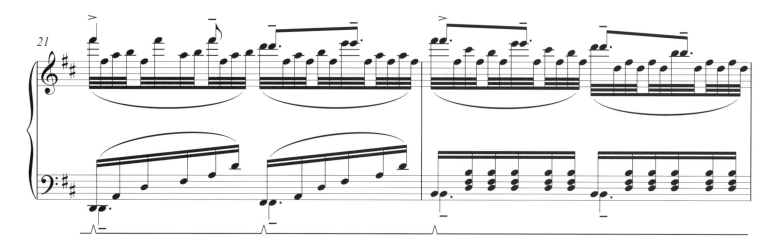

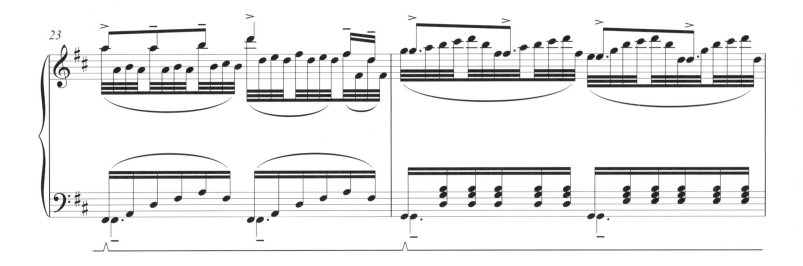

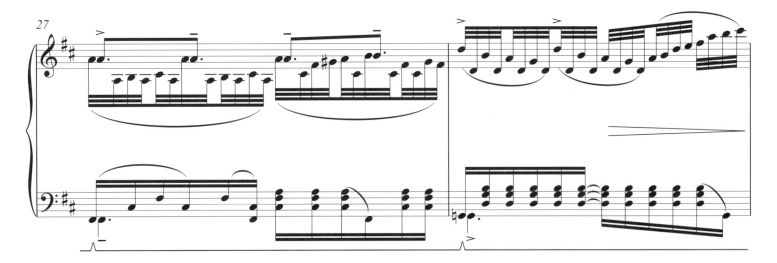

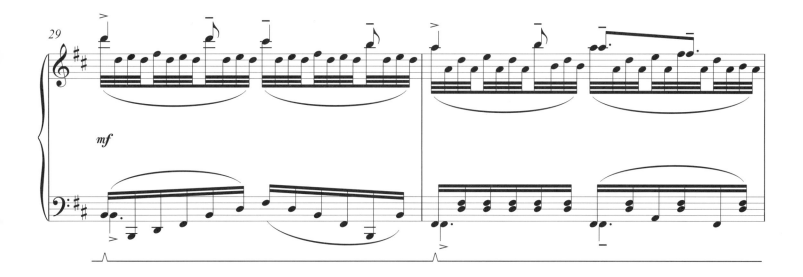

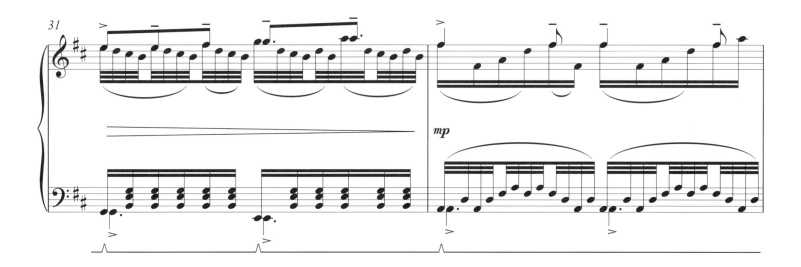

This page was intentionally left blank
to help facilitate page turns.

Bluebird

By Alexis Ffrench

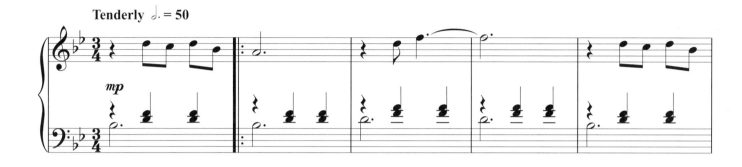

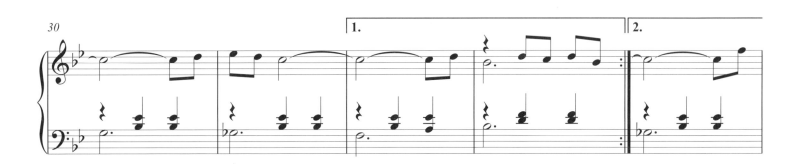

Cinema Paradiso
Love Theme from *Cinema Paradiso*

Music by Ennio Morricone & Andrea Morricone

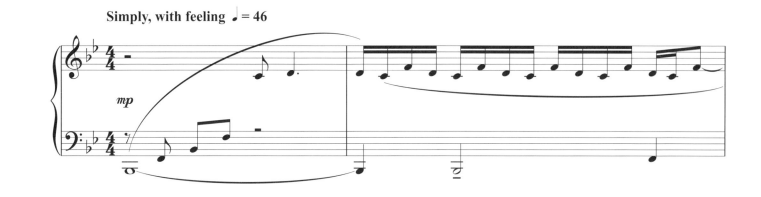

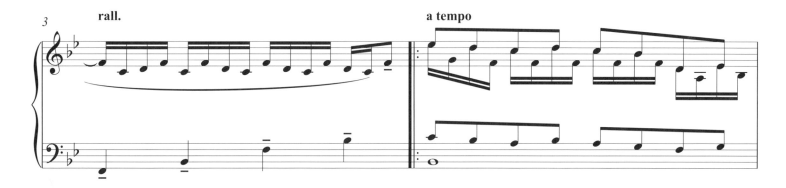

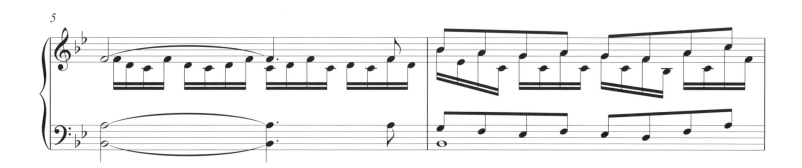

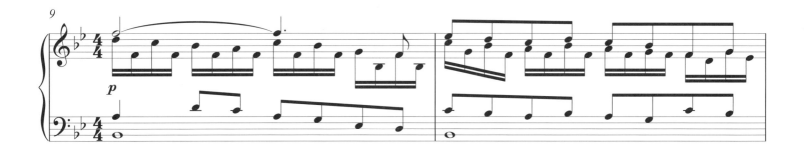

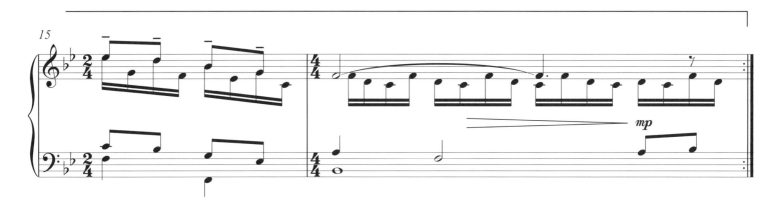

Comptine d'un autre été: L'après-midi

from *Amélie*

Music by Yann Tiersen

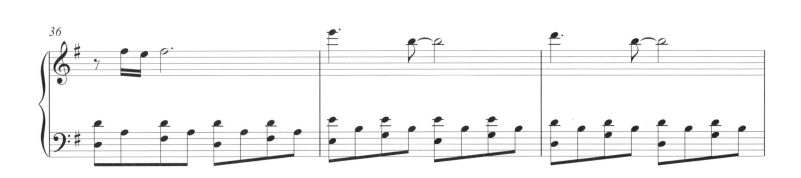

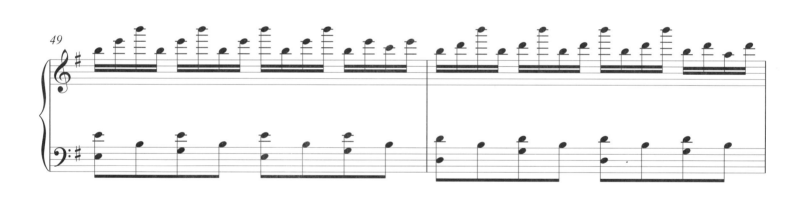

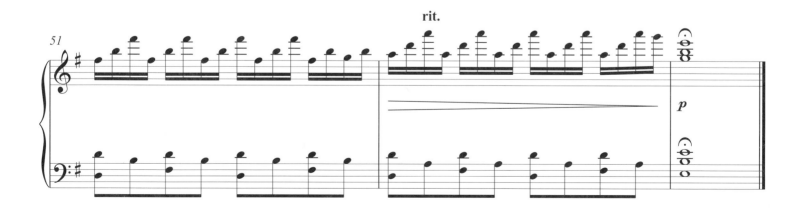

Cavatina

from *The Deer Hunter*

Composed by Stanley Myers

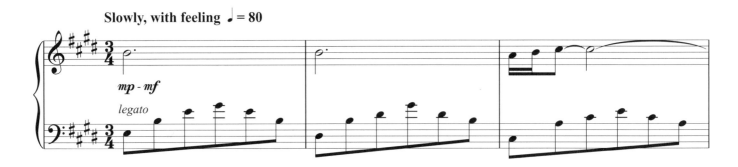

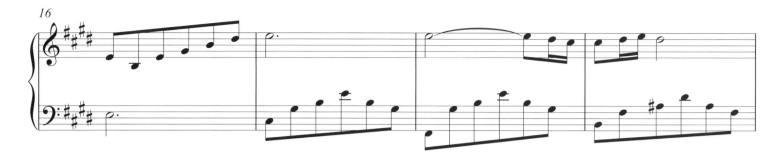

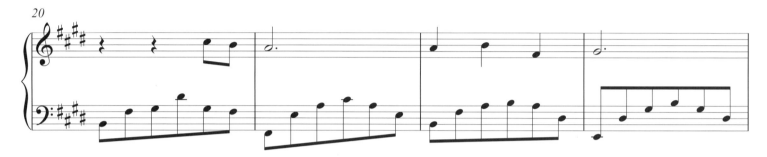

To Coda ⊕

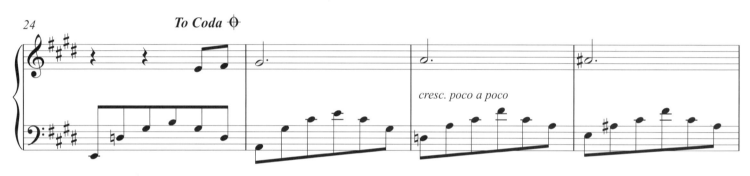

cresc. poco a poco

f

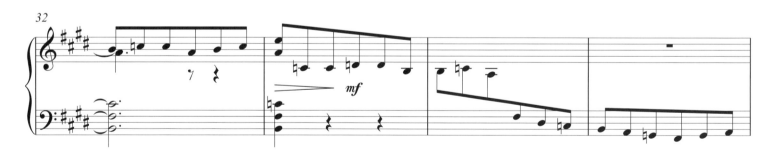

mf

cresc. poco a poco

D.C. al Coda

Coda

poco rit.

molto rit.

Eyes Closed and Travelling

Music by Peter Broderick

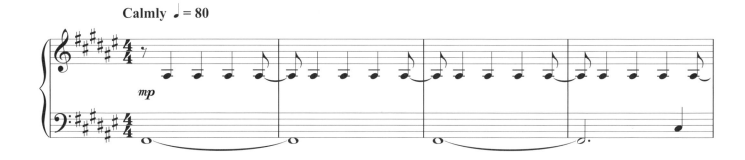

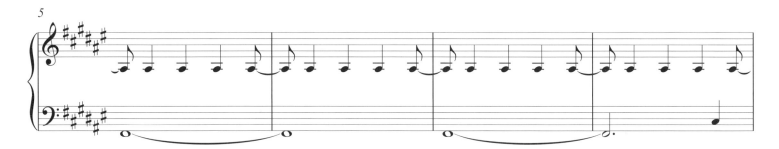

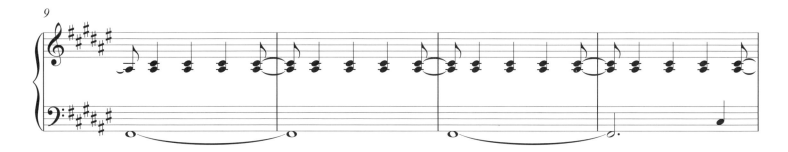

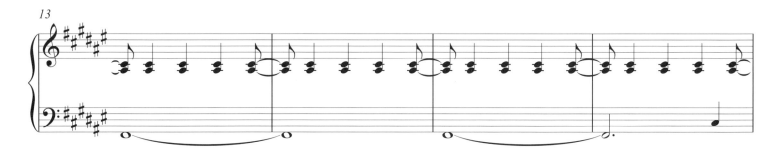

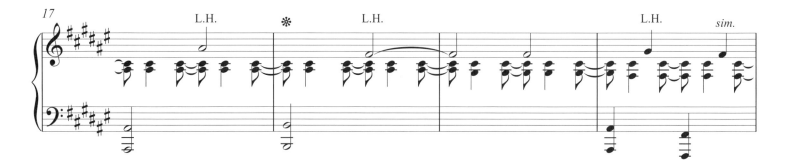

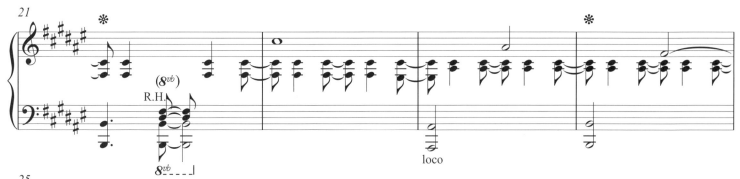

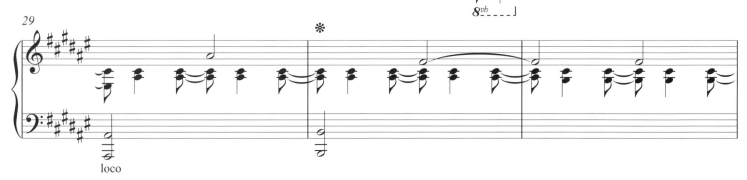

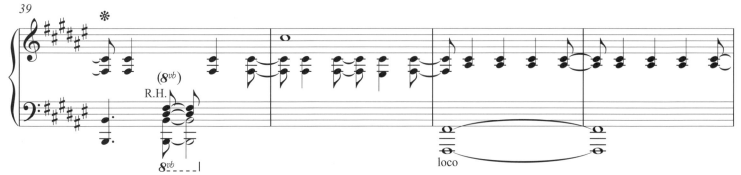

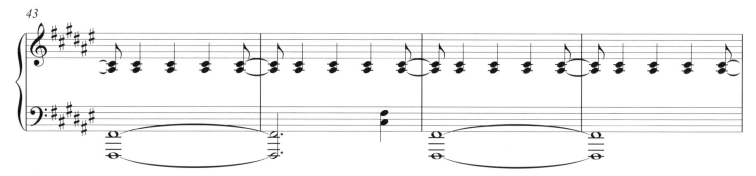

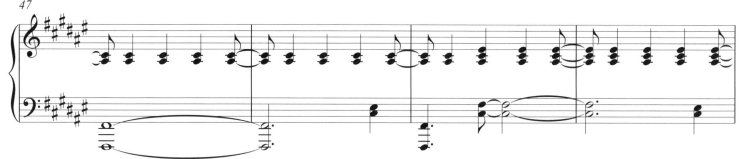

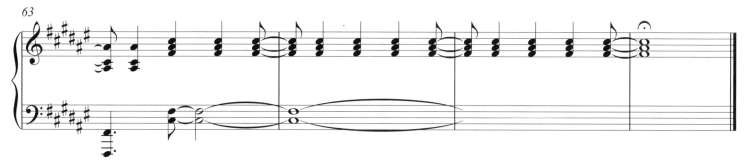

Dalur (Island Songs V)

Music by Ólafur Arnalds

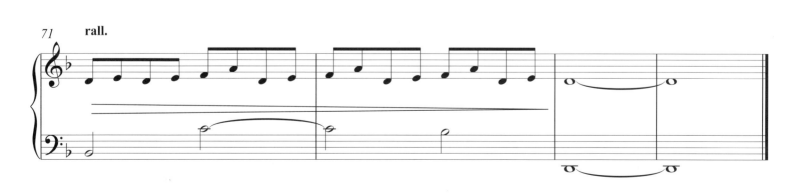

Dawn

from *Pride & Prejudice*

Music by Dario Marianelli

Freely

Moderately slow, very expressively ♩ = 64

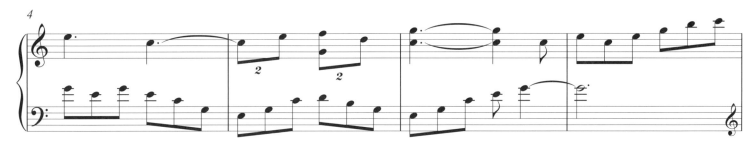

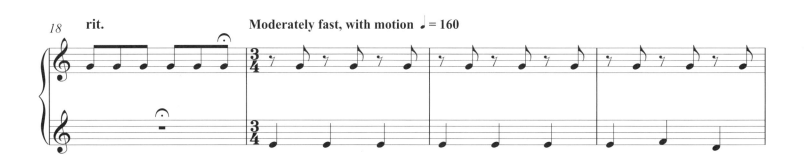

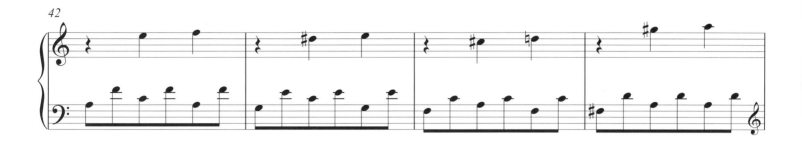

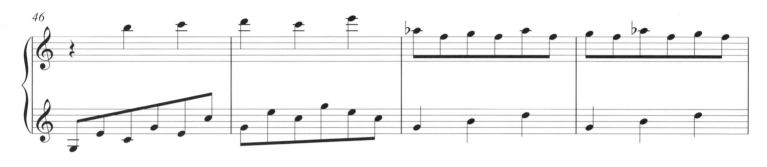

Slightly slower

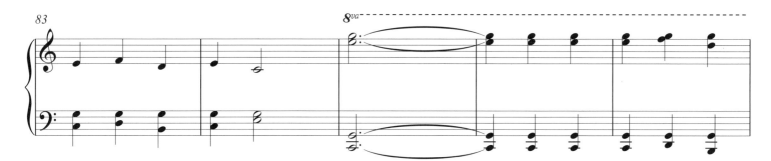

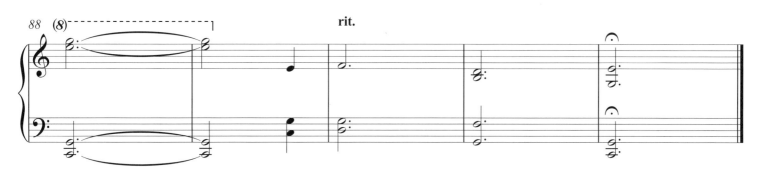

Fly

Music by Ludovico Einaudi

♩ = 112 **Andante con moto**

Piano sample (continue throughout)

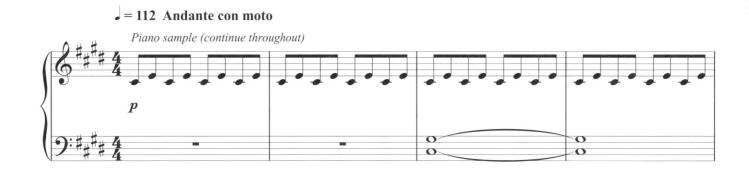

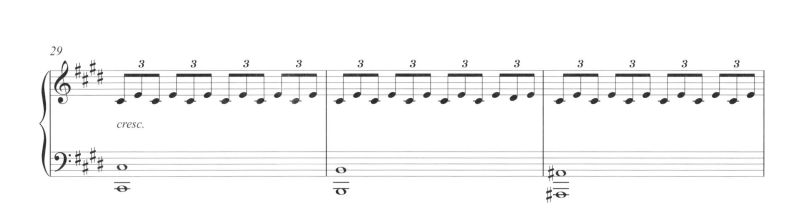

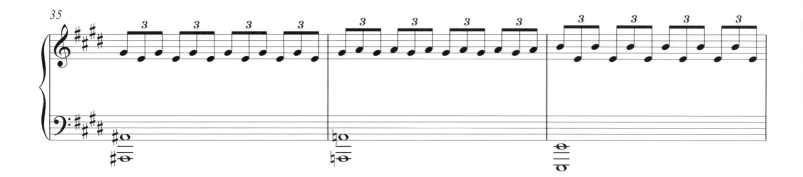

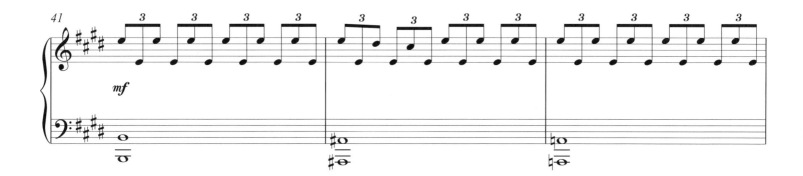

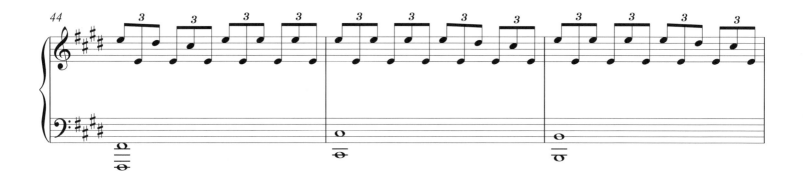

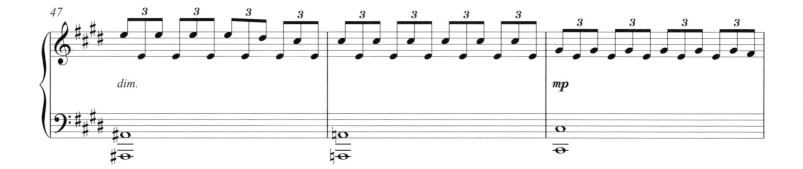

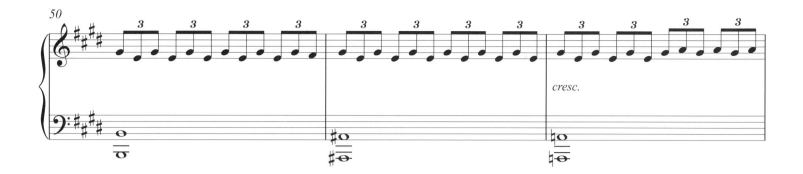

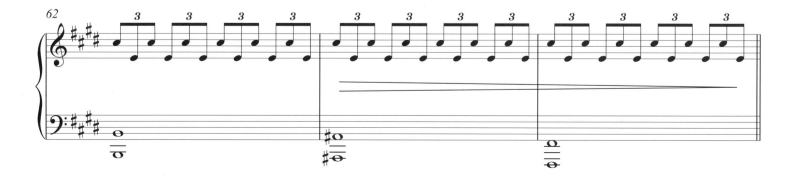

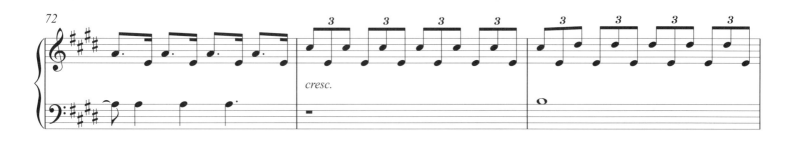

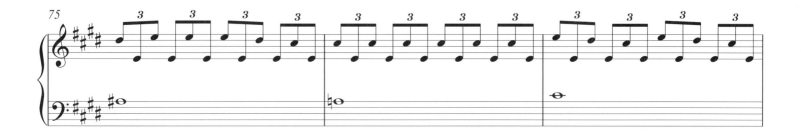

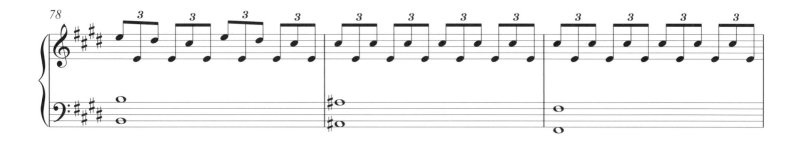

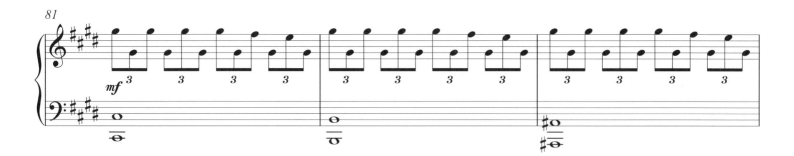

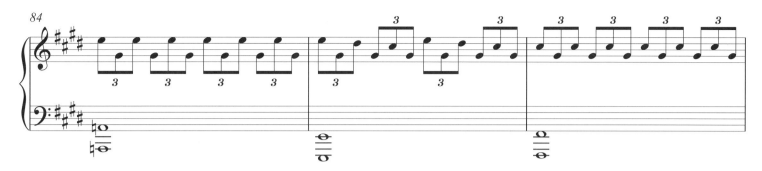

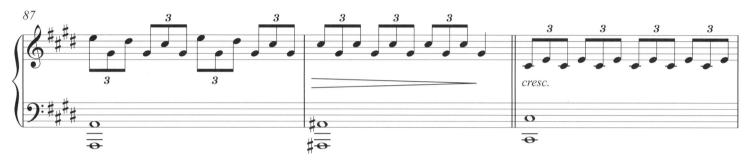

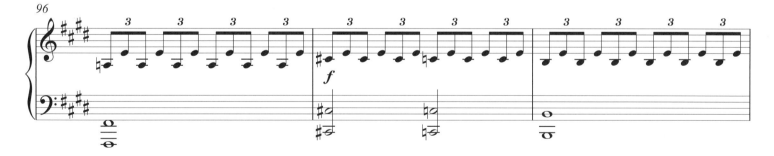

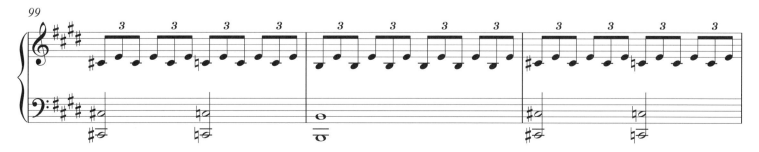

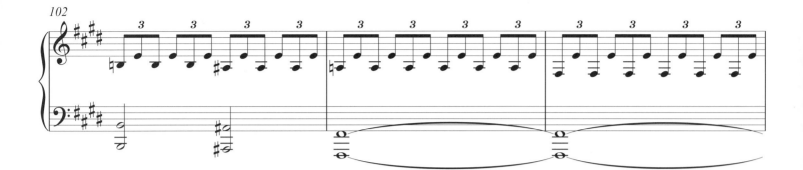

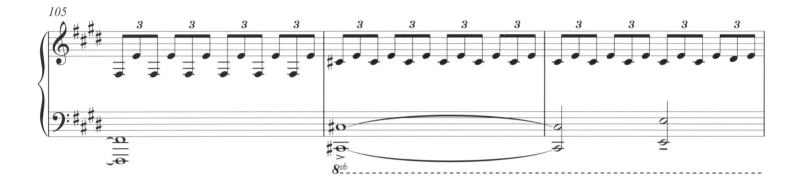

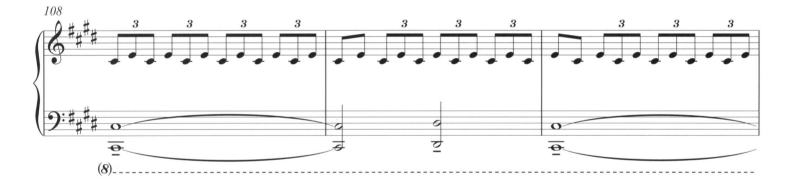

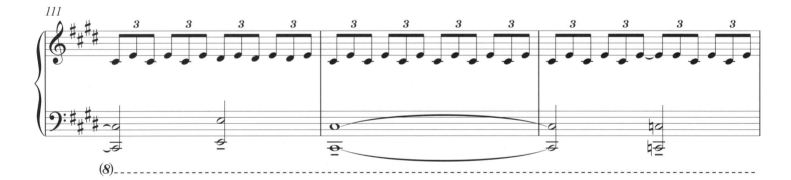

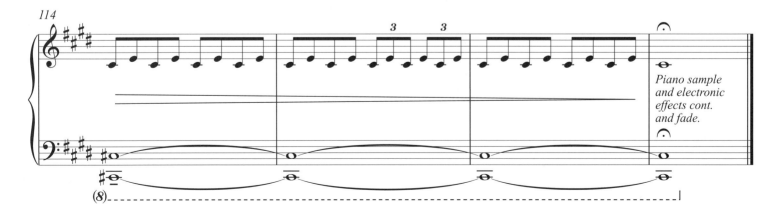

Piano sample and electronic effects cont. and fade.

A Game of Badminton

from *Jane Eyre*

Music by Dario Marianelli

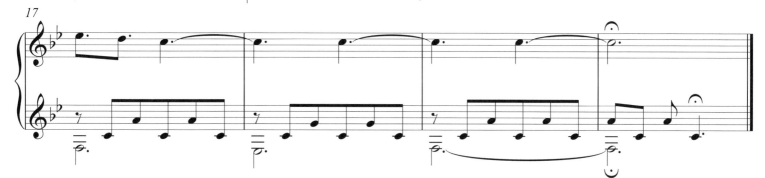

Gizeh

Music by Oskar Schuster

To Coda ⊕

D.C. al Coda   ⊕ Coda

Glasgow Love Theme

from *Love Actually*

Music by Craig Armstrong

Slowly, very freely ♩ = 58

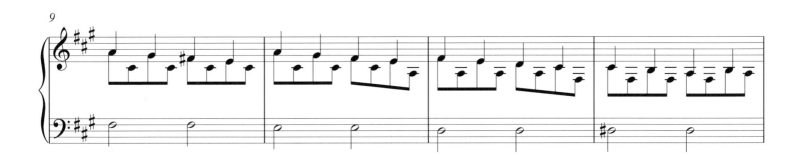

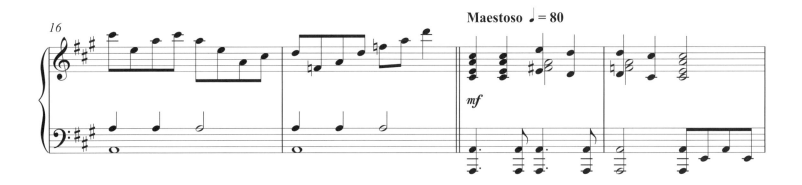

Maestoso ♩= 80

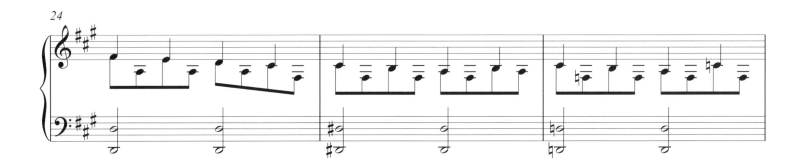

rall.

Grace

Music by Neil Cowley

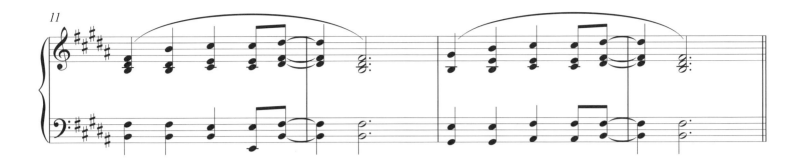

Poco con moto   **Free**

Calm ♩ = *c.* **80**

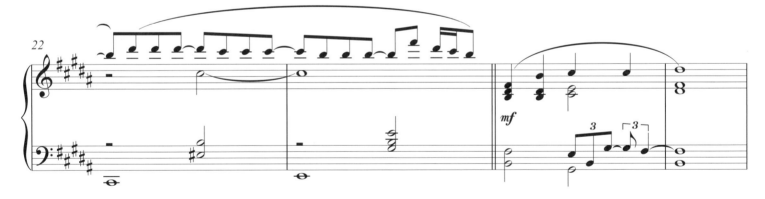

Poco con moto

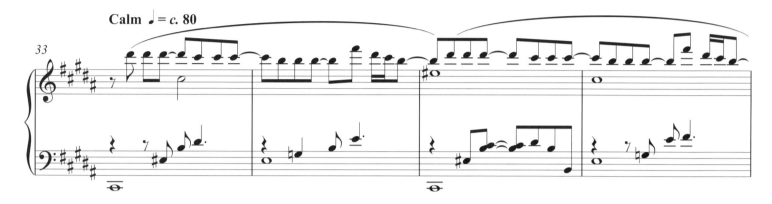

Home
from *The Beauty Inside*

Music by Dustin O'Halloran

Lento ♩ = 56

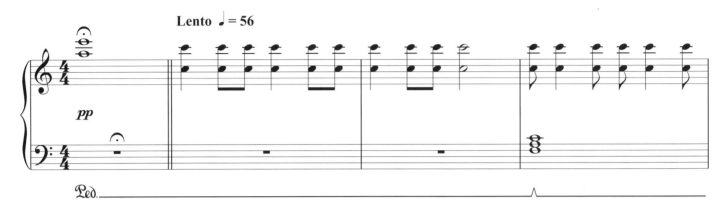

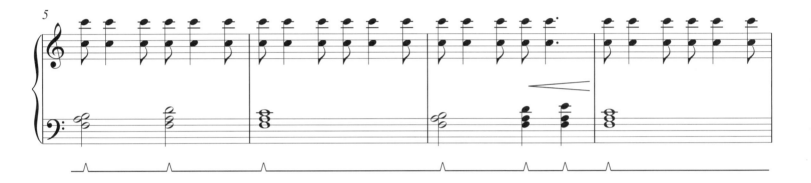

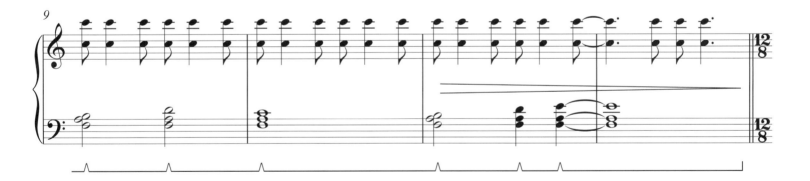

Flowing freely ♩. = 90

In the Morning Light

Words & Music by John Yanni Christopher

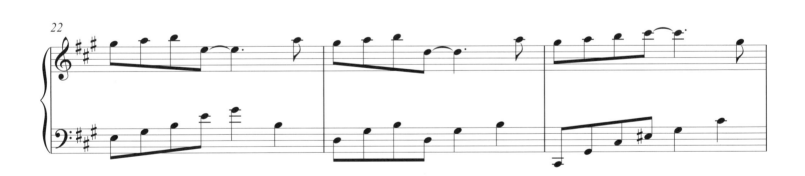

With animation

Kebnekajse

Music by Jeff Larossi & Andreas Romdhane

At a moderate tempo ♩ = 100

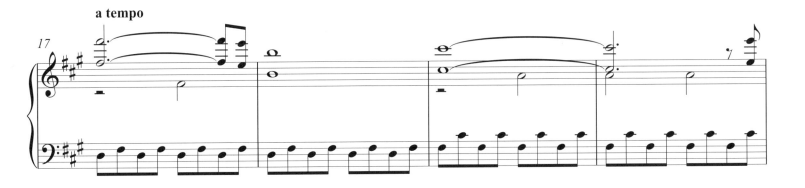

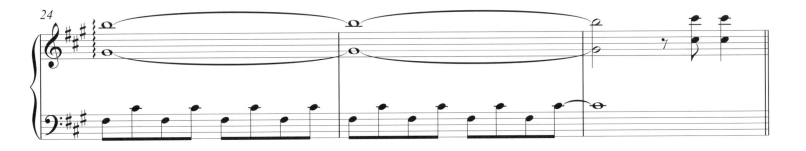

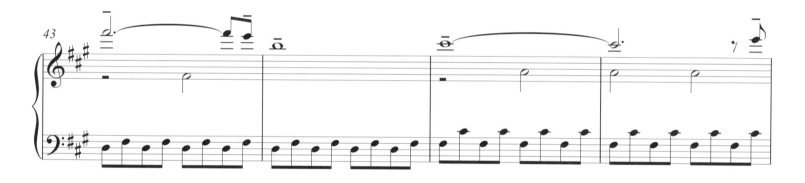

Light of the Seven

from *Game of Thrones*

Music by Ramin Djawadi

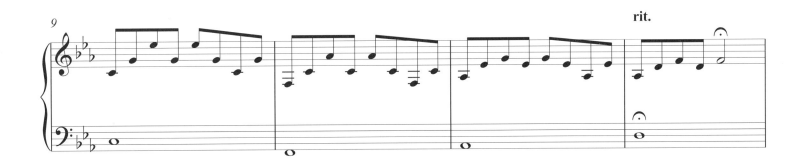

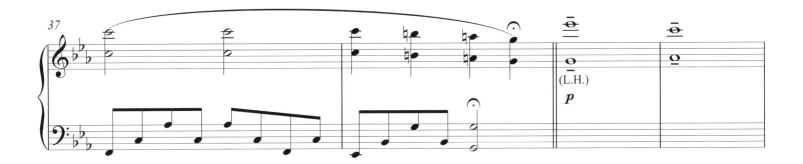

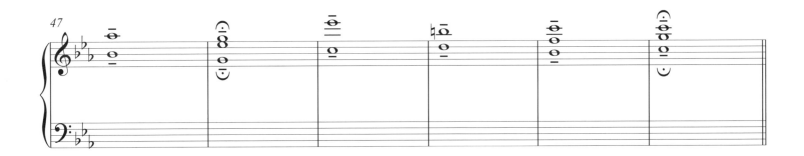

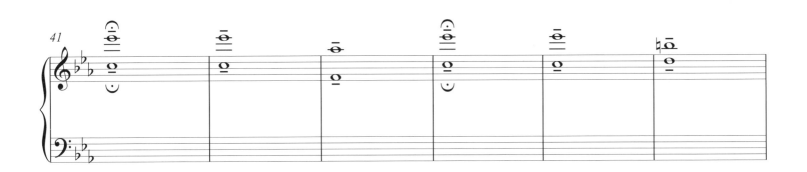

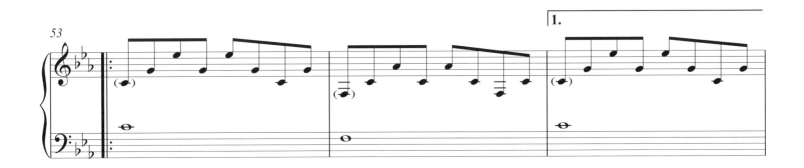

Metamorphosis Two

Composed by Philip Glass

Flowing (♩ = 96–104)

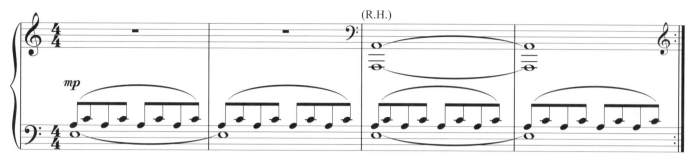

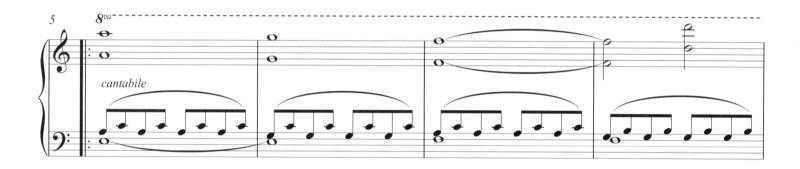

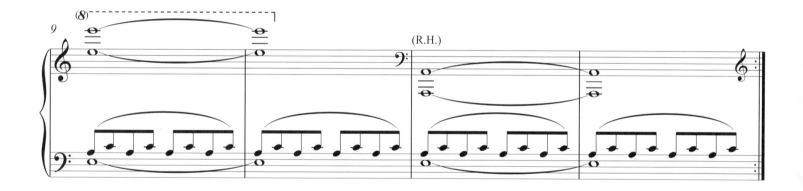

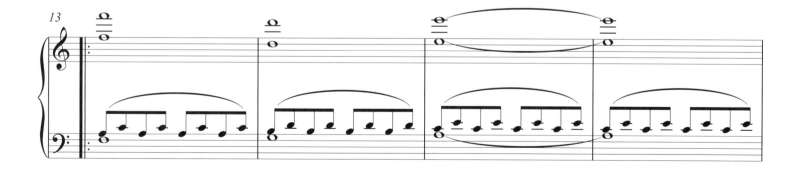

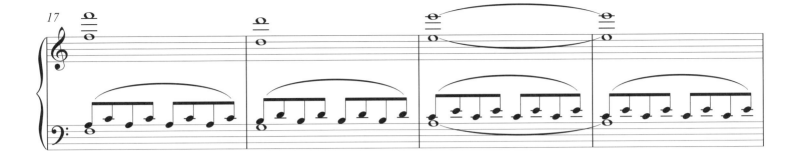

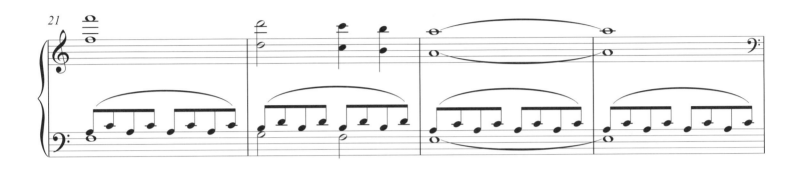

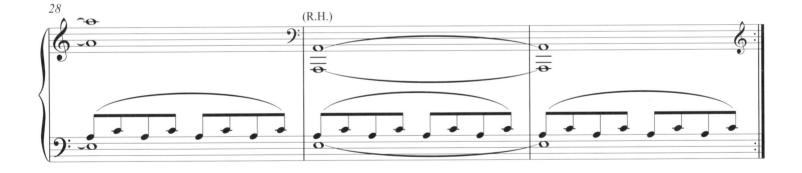

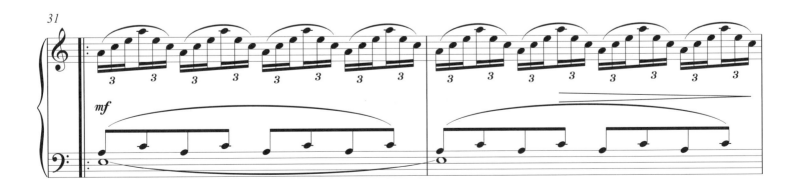

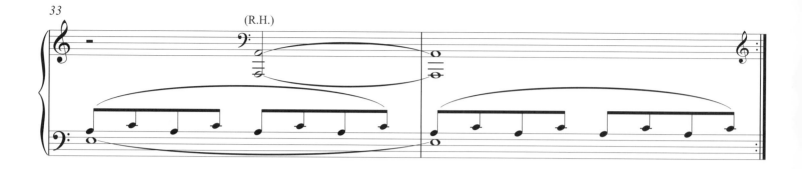

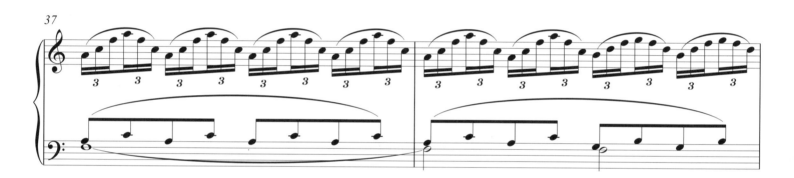

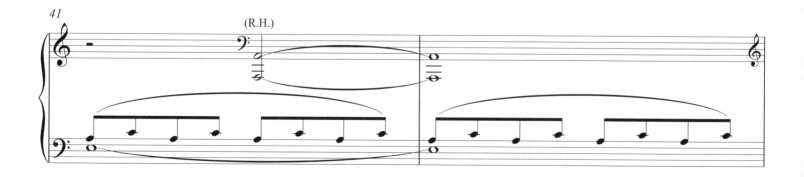

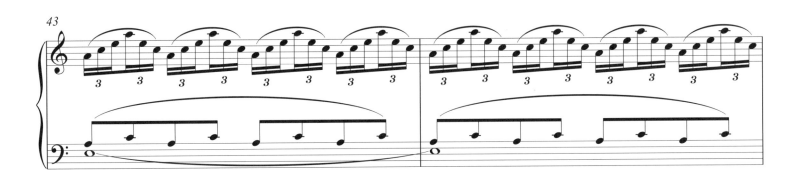

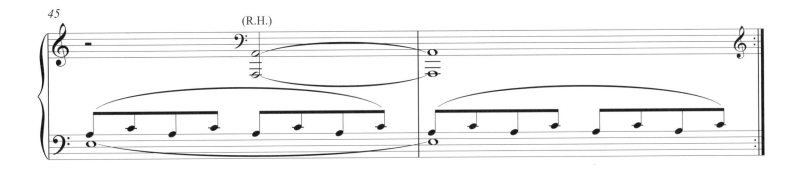

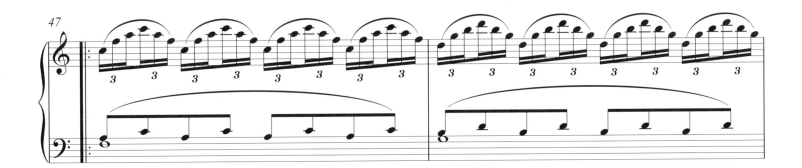

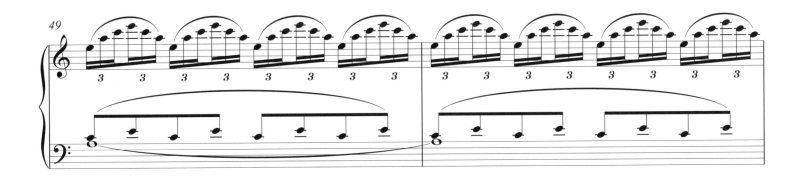

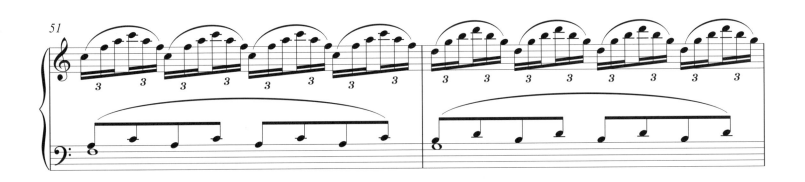

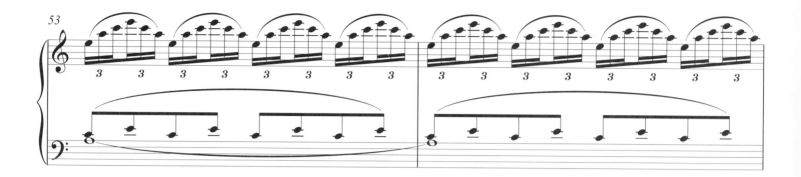

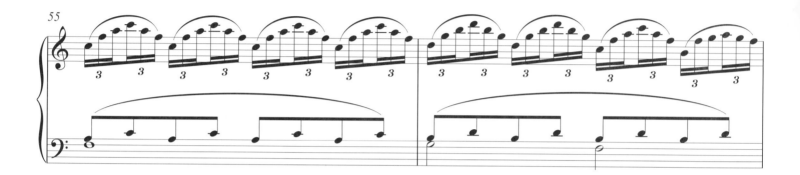

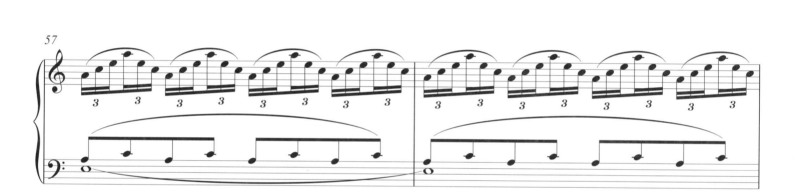

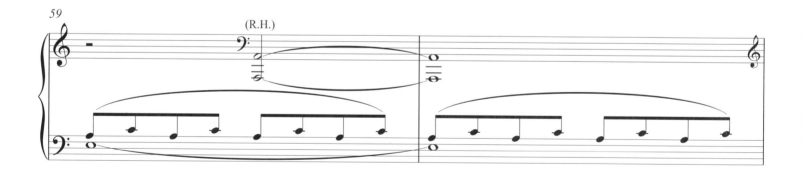

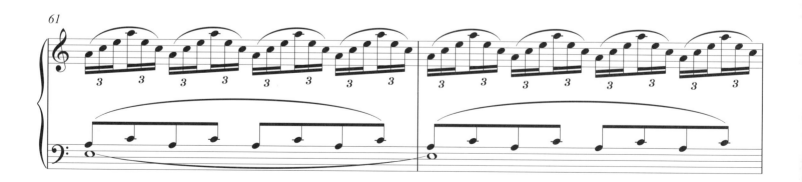

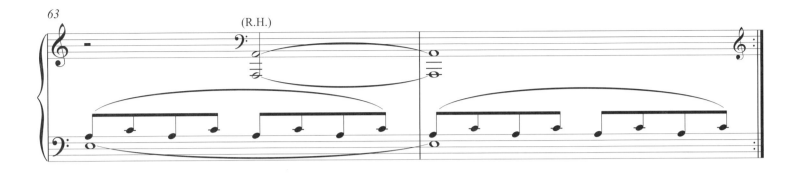

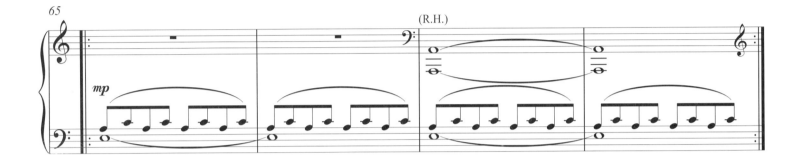

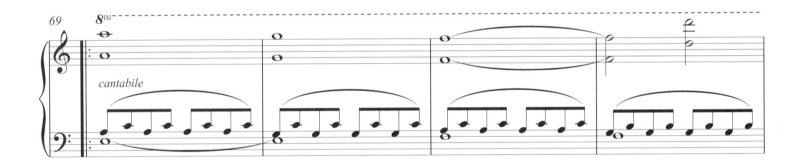

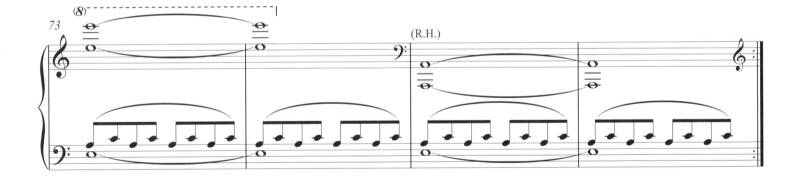

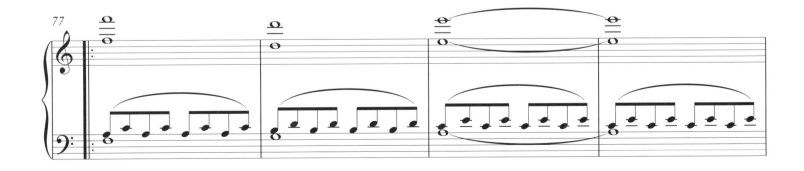

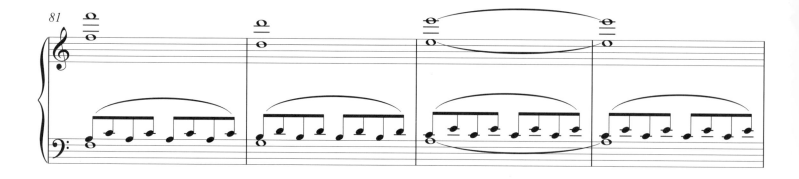

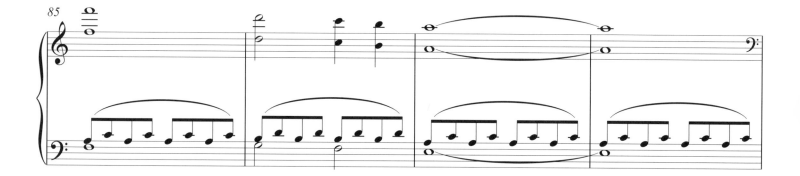

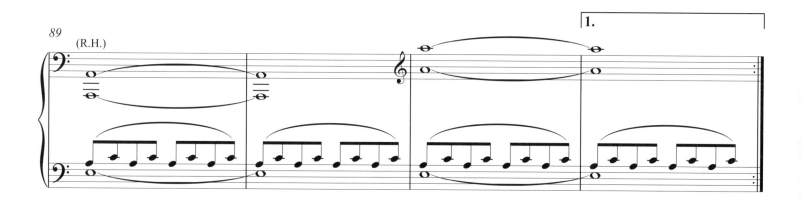

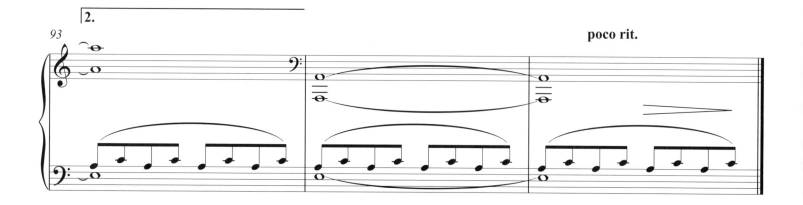

A Model of the Universe

from *The Theory of Everything*

Music by Jóhann Jóhannsson

Somewhere in Time

Theme from *Somewhere in Time*

Music by John Barry

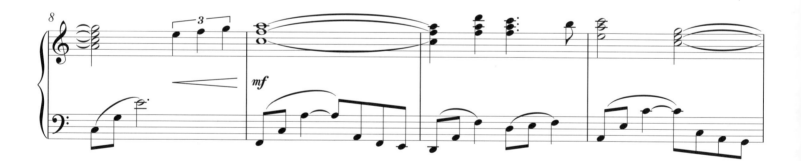

Opening

from *Glassworks*

Music by Philip Glass

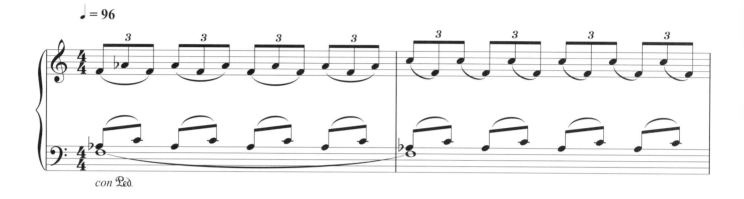

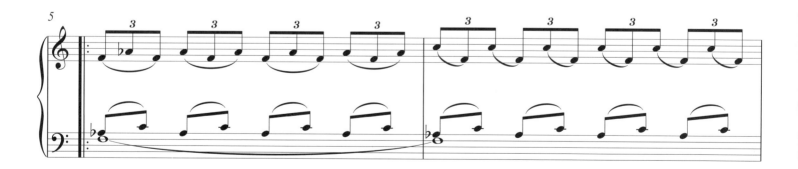

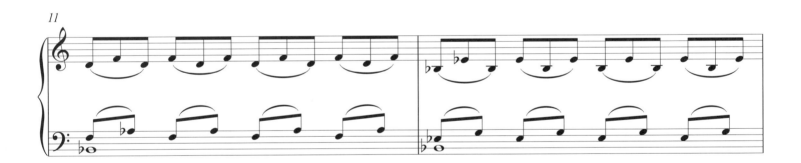

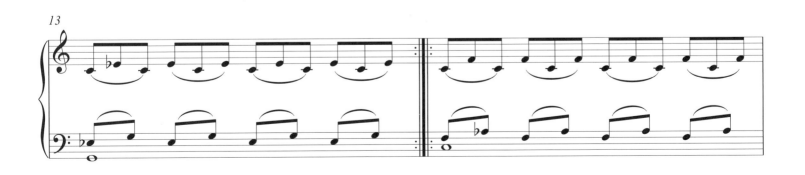

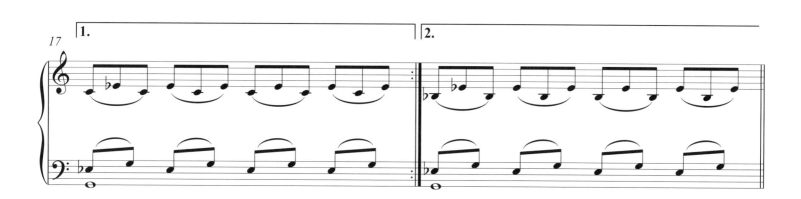

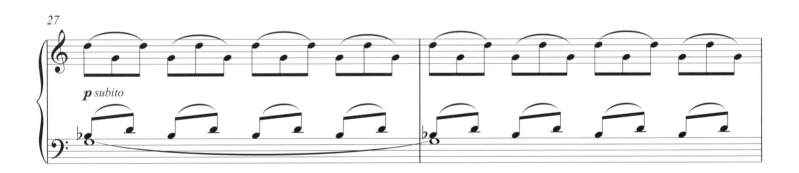

D.C. twice

Opus 23

Music by Dustin O'Halloran

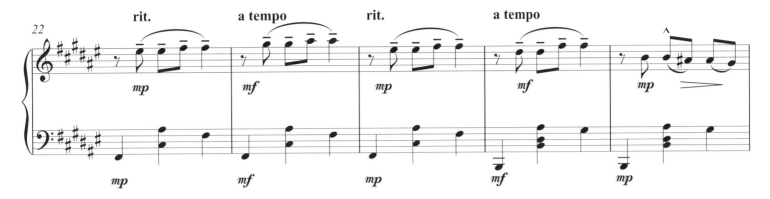

A Time for Us

Love Theme from *Romeo & Juliet*

Words by Larry Kusik & Eddie Snyder
Music by Nino Rota

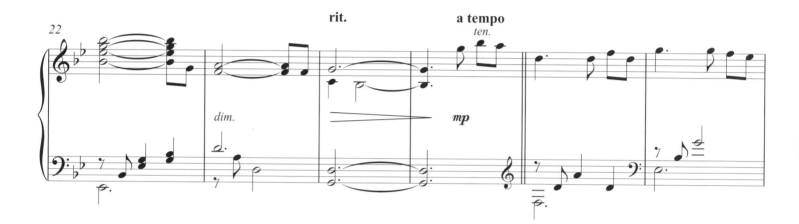

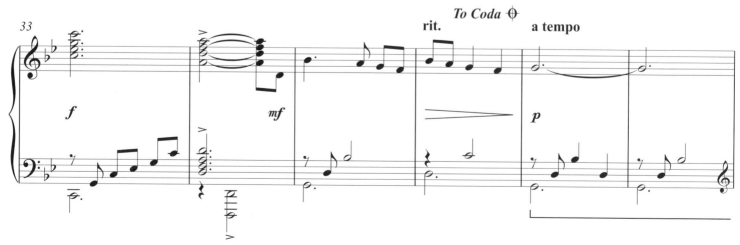

D.S. al Coda

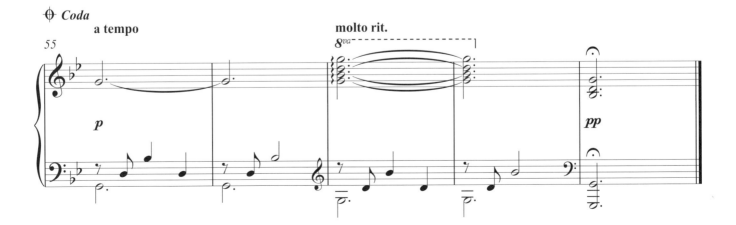

Tokka

Music by Agnes Obel

Travelling

Music by James Spiteri

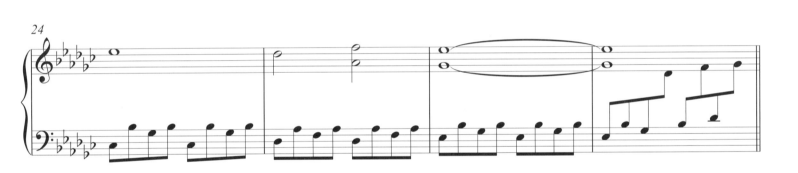

rall.

a tempo

Una Mattina

Music by Ludovico Einaudi

♩ = 80 leggero

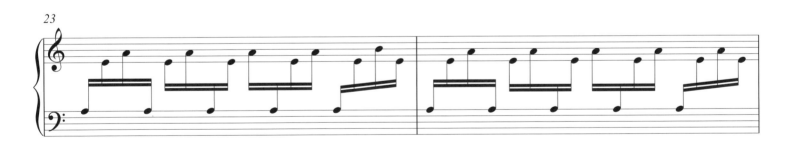

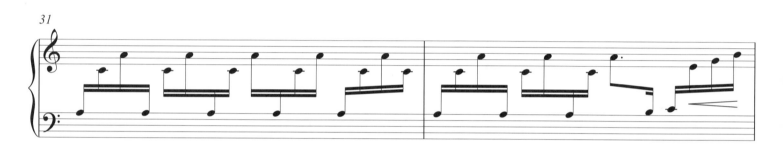

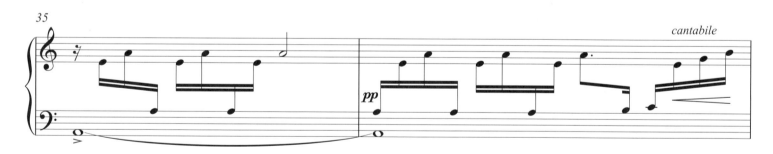

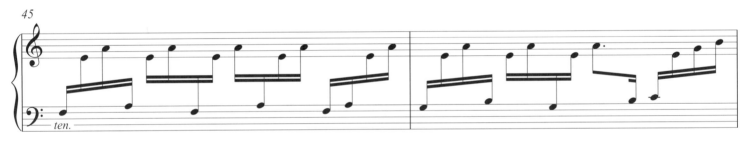

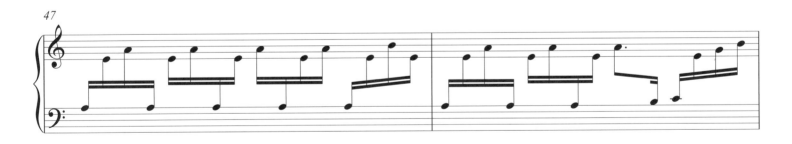

Vladimir's Blues

Music by Max Richter

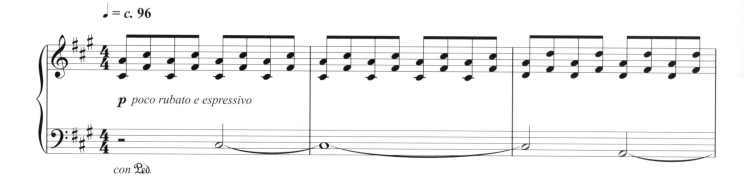

cresc. poco a poco

mp   *mf*

mp   *dim. poco a poco*

poco rit

pp

Watermark

Words & Music by Enya, Roma Ryan & Nicky Ryan

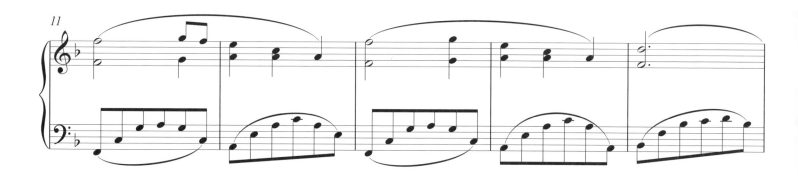

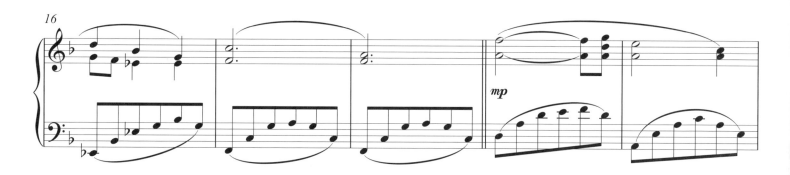

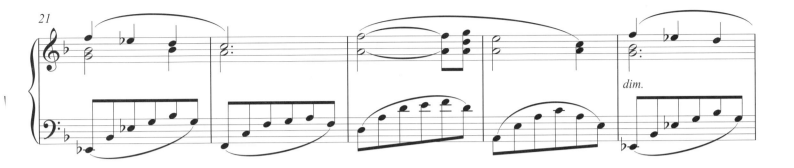

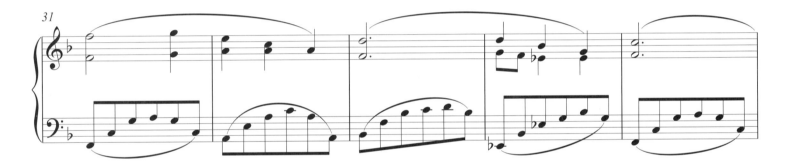

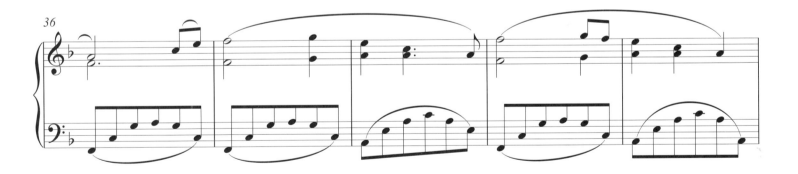

poco rall.

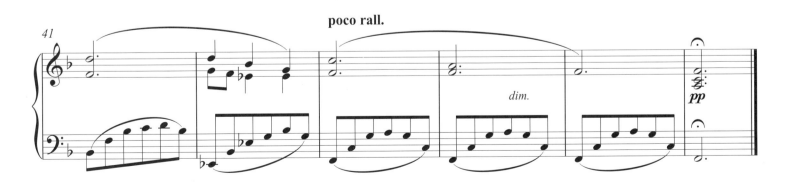

Written on the Sky

Music by Max Richter